Dream

COLORING BOOK

Miryam Adatto

DOVER PUBLICATIONS, INC.
MINEOLA, NEW YORK

Copyright

Copyright © 2017 by Dover Publications, Inc.
All rights reserved.

Bibliographical Note

Dream Coloring Book: Your Passport to Calm is a new work, first published by
Dover Publications, Inc., in 2017.

International Standard Book Number
ISBN-13: 978-0-486-81594-7
ISBN-10: 0-486-81594-3

Manufactured in China by RR Donnelley
81594301   2017
www.doverpublications.com

bliss

\\'blis\\

noun

1. supreme happiness; utter joy or contentment

2. heaven; paradise

3. your passport to calm

Take a pleasant journey into a world of relaxation with *BLISS Dream Coloring Book: Your Passport to Calm*. This delightful treasury of 46 beautiful illustrations includes a variety of graceful birds, lush landscapes, fanciful faces, and other dreamy images sure to immerse you in a state of delightful tranquillity as you color. Now you can travel to your newly found retreat of peace and serenity whenever you'd like with this petite-sized collection of sophisticated artwork.

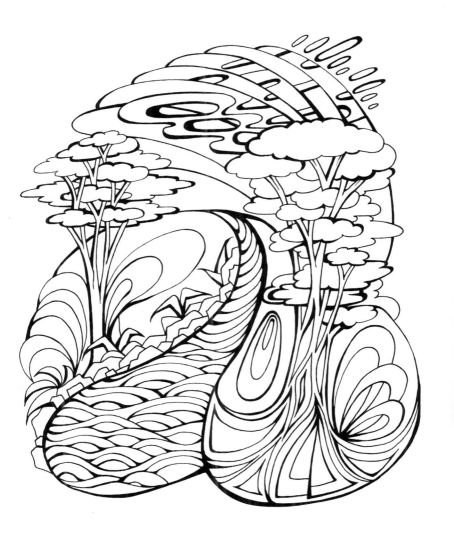

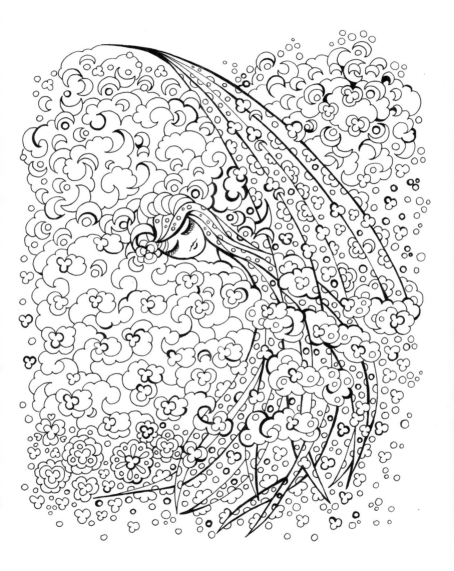